CREATE THE CODE

THE INTERNET

Max Wainewright

All inquiries should be addressed to:
Peterson's Publishing, LLC
4380 S. Syracuse Street, Suite 200
Denver, CO 80237-2624
www.petersonsbooks.com

ISBN: 978-1-4380-8921-8
Printed and bound in China

MIX
Paper from
responsible sources
FSC® C104740

Picture credits:
iStock: fotosipsak: 24; Shutterstock:
Oleksiy Mark: 25.

Every effort has been made to clear
copyright. Should there be any inadvertent
omission, please apply to the publisher for
rectification.

We recommend that children are supervised at
all times when using the Internet. Some of the
projects in this series use a computer webcam or
microphone. Please make sure children are made
aware that they should only allow a computer
to access the webcam or microphone on specific
websites that a trusted adult has told them to
use. We do not recommend children use websites
or microphones on any websites other than those
mentioned in this book.

The website addresses (URLs) included in this book
were valid at the time of going to press. However,
it is possible that contents or addresses may have
changed since the publication of this book. No
responsibility for any such changes can be accepted
by either the author or the Publisher.

Contents

For help with any of
the projects go to:
www.maxw.com

The Internet

The first computers were much slower, simpler, and less sophisticated than even the most basic mobile phones we have today. But the big difference in today's computers, tablets, and phones are their ability to connect to each other.

This gives us access to almost all the information, music, books, videos, and games available today no matter where we are on the planet. But how does this connectivity work?

Connected Computers

During the 1960s, various university, military, and research laboratories started to explore ways to connect computers to each other. This led to various innovations for connecting computers, and the invention of the **Network**. ARPANET was created in 1969 and is considered to be the first ever network.

A network is a group of two or more computers connected to each other for sharing things. Early networks used cables. Today many networks are wireless.

The Internet

At the beginning of 1983, a standard for how networks worked was agreed. It was called TCP/IP. It made it possible to connect networks from around the world. This network of networks was called the **Internet**.

When computers are in the same building, they can be connected through cables. To connect computers in different cities or countries, other techniques are used. Early networks sent computer data (information) through telephone cables as a series of very fast beeps. Other computers decoded the beeps to turn them back into data.

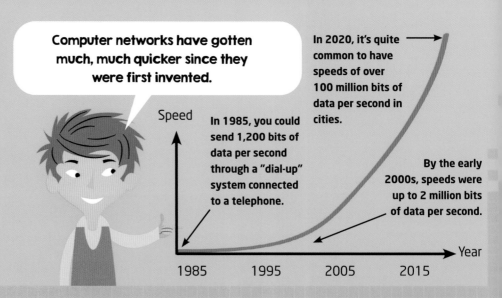

Computer networks have gotten much, much quicker since they were first invented.

Speed

In 1985, you could send 1,200 bits of data per second through a "dial-up" system connected to a telephone.

In 2020, it's quite common to have speeds of over 100 million bits of data per second in cities.

By the early 2000s, speeds were up to 2 million bits of data per second.

Year

1985   1995   2005   2015

A Worldwide Network

The development of the Internet meant it was possible to access information from other computers around the world. But it was still quite tricky to do. In the late 1980s, an English scientist called Tim Berners-Lee developed ideas to make the Internet easier to use.

Tim Berners-Lee came up with a number of inventions that, when combined, make up the **World Wide Web**:

▶ A way to say **where information is stored** called URLs, short for Universal Resource Locators, also known as web addresses.

▶ A special **coding language to create pages of information** with links to other pages called HTML (HyperText Markup Language).

▶ A **system to share the pages** over the Internet called HTTP (HyperText Transfer Protocol).

> Tim also invented the first ever web browser. He later called it Nexus.

> A web browser is the app we use to view web pages. Google Chrome, Safari, and Firefox are all browsers.

> In this book we will learn to use HTML.

People tend to use the words Internet and web to mean the same thing. To computer scientists and coders, the Internet is about network connections and computers—hardware. The web is really the coding languages, techniques, and data that travel across the Internet, bringing it to life.

An Evolving Network

The way we use computer connectivity continues to change everyday. Using cables to connect to the Internet was quite restrictive. So now, instead of cables we use wireless WiFi to connect devices to the Internet. As well as connecting computers, the Internet now connects to cars, cameras, and even fridges! In the future, it may even connect computers and robots directly to human beings. But web pages still rely on HTML and the ideas Berners-Lee developed. In this book you'll find out more about how these technologies work and learn how to use HTML and JavaScript to build web pages. Let's get started!

How Data Travels

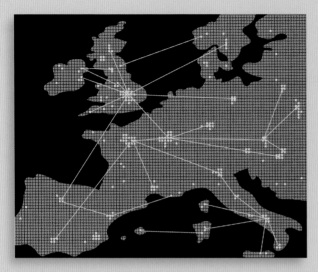

Let's find out a bit more about how data travels through the Internet. If you are looking at a website, the data in the form of pictures, text, video, and sounds on it are split up into tiny sections. Each section is called a data packet.

When you visit a website, hundreds or thousands of data packets will be sent to your computer.

A picture will be broken down into a number of separate packets.

So that each packet knows where it is going, it is given an IP address.

When packets arrive they are put back together in the correct order.

How much data?

1 0
Any data stored on a computer is broken down into a series of 1s and 0s. These are known as bits of information.

10010111

8 bits are combined together to create a byte. A byte uses a way of counting called binary. This allows it to store a number between 0 and 255.

1000* bytes combine together to make a kilobyte or KB. A KB is big enough to store a typical paragraph of text.

1000 KB make one megabyte (MB). A megabyte can store a photo.

1000 MB make one gigabyte (GB). A gigabyte can store around 20 minutes of high-quality video.

*A KB used to be 1024 bytes of data, but now a KB counts as 1000 bytes.

You can test out how data packets travel to and from your computer by using a program called ping.

STEP 1: Start the command prompt

On a PC:

Hold down the Windows key on the keyboard.

R

Tap the **R** key.

Run

cmd

OK

The **Run** window will appear. Type cmd then click **OK**.

On a Mac:

cmd ⌘

Hold down the command key on the keyboard.

Tap the space bar.

🔍 terminal

The spotlight search bar will appear. Type **terminal** then press **Enter**.

STEP 2: Ping a website

Type in **ping** followed by a website address and press enter.

ping google.com

You don't need to type www or http.

STEP 3: View results

The results of your ping test will appear:

```
PING google.com (216.58.210.206): 56 data bytes
64 bytes from 216.58.210.206: icmp_seq=0 ttl=55 time=22.708 ms
64 bytes from 216.58.210.206: icmp_seq=1 ttl=55 time=14.355 ms
64 bytes from 216.58.210.206: icmp_seq=2 ttl=55 time=11.527 ms
64 bytes from 216.58.210.206: icmp_seq=3 ttl=55 time=11.993 ms
64 bytes from 216.58.210.206: icmp_seq=4 ttl=55 time=11.528 ms
```

The size of the data packet.

This tells us how many networks the data packet has passed through.

How long it took the data packet to travel in milliseconds.

Ctrl **C** Hold down Ctrl and tap C to stop the ping test.

EXPERIMENT

Try pinging different websites. Which one has the fastest response? Which is the slowest? Which one passes through the most networks?

Editing HTML Code

For the projects in this book, we will be using fairly advanced coding techniques. You will need to download a program called a text editor to create the code for these projects.

Visit www.maxw.com for more info on downloading text editors.

STEP 1: Go to the Sublime Text website

www.sublimetext.com

Sublime Text

Open your web browser and visit **www.sublimetext.com**.

STEP 2: Download

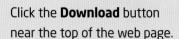

Download

Click the **Download** button near the top of the web page.

Choose the version you need.

OSX (10.7 or later)
Windows—also
Windows 64 bit

STEP 3: Install the software

Some web browsers will then ask you to run the installation program. Choose "Run."

Installing ...

If this does not happen, don't panic. The installer file should have been downloaded to your computer. Look in your **downloads** folder for it. Double-click on it to start installing your new text editor. You should get a gray box giving you instructions on what to do next. Follow these instructions to complete the installation.

STEP 4: Running Sublime Text

Open **Sublime Text** from your app list.

STEP 5: A simple web page

Carefully type this into your text editor.

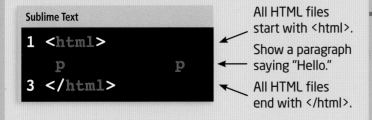

```
Sublime Text
1  <html>
     p                    p
3  </html>
```

All HTML files start with <html>.

Show a paragraph saying "Hello."

All HTML files end with </html>.

STEP 6: Save your page

- Click **File > Save**.
- Go to your documents folder.
- Type **hello.html** as the file name.

STEP 7: View your page

- Open your documents folder.
- Find the **hello.html** file and double-click on it.
- Your web page should now load in your normal web browser.

documents/hello.html

Hello

Now you have built a simple web page we will learn how to use it to make more complex ones.

<tags>

Tags always start with < and end with > (known as angle brackets). All elements have an opening tag and most have a closing tag.

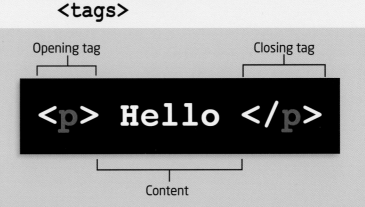

Opening tag

Closing tag

<p> Hello </p>

Content

Your Favorites

We will start by making a simple web page which shows a list of your favorite things.

As well as using the paragraph tag again, we will learn to use some new tags. The <h1> heading tag is used to show a main title, and the <h2> tag as a smaller heading.

STEP 1: Start a new HTML file
Start your text editor or click **File > New**.

All web pages start with doctype and html tags . . .

STEP 2: Type in the code
Type this code into your text editor.

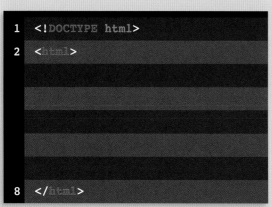

```
1  <!DOCTYPE html>
2  <html>




8  </html>
```

← Set the document type.
← Start the HTML page.
← The main heading.
← A smaller (sub) heading.

Three separate paragraphs listing your favorite sports.

← The end of the HTML page.

. . . and they all end with the closing html tag.

STEP 3: Save the page
- Click **File > Save**.
- Go to your documents folder.
- Type **fav.html** as the file name.

STEP 4: View your page
- Open your documents folder and double-click on the **fav.html** file.

Your web page should look like this.

documents/fav.html

My Favorite Things
My Favorite Sports:
Soccer
Trampolining
Swimming

STEP 5: Arrange your screen

It's useful to see your HTML code and web page in the web browser at the same time. Many web developers set up their screen with the code on the left side and their web page on the right side. Resize your text editor and browser windows so your screen looks like this:

```
1    <!DOCTYPE html>
2    <html>



8    </html>
```

documents/fav.html

My Favorite Things
My Favorite Sports:
Soccer
Trampolining
Swimming

To see the effects of your changes, you need to reload the web page by clicking the refresh icon.

After you have made a change to your HTML code in the text editor, save your file.

Now add another list— your favorite foods.

STEP 6: Make space

```
8    </html>
```

Click at the start of line 8.

```
8
9    </html>
```

Press the enter key to make a gap.

```
8
9    </html>
```

Click at the start of line 8 again.

STEP 7: Enter more HTML

Add four more lines starting at line 8.

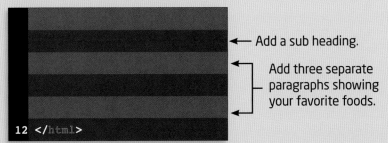

```
12   </html>
```

← Add a sub heading.

Add three separate paragraphs showing your favorite foods.

STEP 8: See the changes

Save your work again, then refresh your web page. See step 5 for help.

EXPERIMENT

Add more lists—maybe your favorite movies, songs, or TV programs.

Color and Shape—Bake A Cake

Let's create a page for a cake store, drawing cakes using layers of colored rectangles with rounded corners.

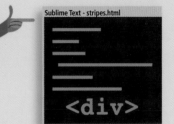

Instead of using paragraphs we will use an HTML element called a div—short for division.

STEP 1: Start a new HTML file

Start your text editor or click **File > New**.

Sublime Text - stripes.html

`<div>`

STEP 2: Type in the code

Type this into your text editor. Be careful with the symbols like >/' and ;

```
1  <!DOCTYPE html>
2  <html>
3    <style>
4      div{width:400px; border-radius:5px;}
5    </style>
6  <h3>Vanilla Cake</h3>
7  <div style='background-color:pink; height:8px;'></div>
8  <div style='background-color:gold; height:70px;'></div>
9  <div style='background-color:red; height:20px;'></div>
10 <div style='background-color:gold; height:70px;'></div>
11 </html>
```

Set the document type.

Start the HTML file.

Start the style section.

Make sure all divs are 400 pixels wide with a curved corner.

End the style section.

Show a medium heading.

Add four separate divs to show the frosting on top of the cake, the top layer of frosting, some frosting for the middle, plus a bottom layer.

End the HTML file.

STEP 3: Save your page

- Click **File > Save**.
- Go to your documents folder.
- Type **cake.html** as the file name.

STEP 4: View your page

- Open your documents folder and double-click on the **cake.html** file.

documents/cake.html

Vanilla cake

Coders often copy and paste lines of code to save time and avoid mistyping.

STEP 5: Add more cake—copy some code

Click here to position your cursor at the start of line 6.

```
6  <h3>Vanilla Cake</h3>
7  <div style='background-color:pink;
8  <div style='background-color:gold; height:70px;'></div>
9  <div style='background-color:red; height:20px;'></div>
10 <div style='background-color:gold; height:70px;'></div>
```

Drag down and right to highlight the line of code.

On a PC, hold down the **Control** key, and tap "**C.**"

On a Mac, hold the **Command** key then tap "**C.**"

STEP 6: Make space and paste your code

Click at the start of line 11.

Press the enter key to make a gap.

Click at the start of line 11 again.

On a PC, hold down the **Control** key, and tap "**V.**"

On a Mac, hold the **Command** key then tap "**V.**"

STEP 7: Edit the new lines of code

Now you will have five extra lines of code:

```
10 <div style='background-color:gold; height:70px;'></div>
11 <h3>Chocolate Cake</h3>
12 <div style='background-color:orange; height:8px;'></div>
13 <div style='background-color:chocolate; height:70px;'></div>
14 <div style='background-color:brown; height:20px;'></div>
15 <div style='background-color:chocolate; height:70px;'></div>
16 </html>
```

Change the heading for your cake from Vanilla to Chocolate Cake.

Change the color words for your cake. Use orange, chocolate, and brown instead of pink, gold, and red.

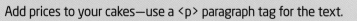

STEP 8: See the changes

Save your work again, then refresh your web page. See step 5 on page 11 for help with this and to arrange your screen.

EXPERIMENT

Add prices to your cakes—use a <p> paragraph tag for the text.

Repeat step 7 to copy and paste another cake. What flavor will it be?

Can you work out how to make a triple-layer cake?

Now that you have designed a few cakes, why not start a cake store? Make up a name for it. Use an <h1> tag to display your store name.

Online Shopping

More and more things can be bought through the Internet. In this project, we'll find out how to set up a web page for an imaginary online store.

Although the web page will allow you to choose what to buy, you'll have to arrange your own imaginary delivery!

STEP 1: New file

Start your text editor or click **File > New**.

We will create a drop-down menu for the store using <select> and <option> tags.

STEP 2: Type in the code

Type this code into your text editor.

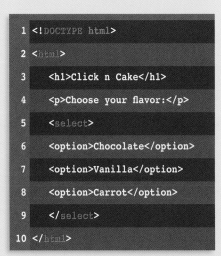

```
1  <!DOCTYPE html>
2  <html>
3      <h1>Click n Cake</h1>
4      <p>Choose your flavor:</p>
5      <select>
6      <option>Chocolate</option>
7      <option>Vanilla</option>
8      <option>Carrot</option>
9      </select>
10 </html>
```

← Set the document type.

← Start the HTML page.

← The main heading.

← Tell customers what to do.

← Start a drop-down element.

← Add an option element for each flavor of cake. This code will create three different options in the drop-down menu.

← The end of the drop-down.

← The end of the HTML page.

Shopping online—How it works

Real online stores use code just like yours to let people choose what to order. Once the order is placed, code runs on the website server to carry out the following steps:

The customer buys an item from the online store.

£ 320619084075

The website communicates with the bank.

@

Emails are sent to the customer and the warehouse.

The ordered item is found in the warehouse.

Mr Customer
11 House Street
London
N10

The item is sent to the customer.

STEP 3: Save the page

- Click **File > Save**.
- Go to your documents folder.
- Type **store.html** as the file name.

STEP 4: View your page

- Open your documents folder and double-click on the **store.html** file.

documents/cake.html

**Click 'n' Cake
Choose your flavor**

Vanilla ▼
Chocolate
Vanilla
Carrot

Try choosing a flavor for your cake.

STEP 5: Add more code

Click near the start of line 10 and press enter to create a blank line. (See page 13, step 6 for help.) Type in the code below:

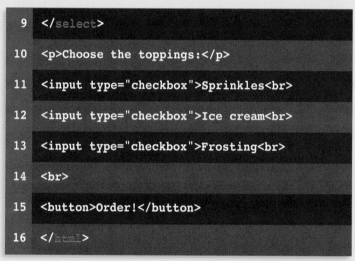

```
 9   </select>

10   <p>Choose the toppings:</p>

11   <input type="checkbox">Sprinkles<br>

12   <input type="checkbox">Ice cream<br>

13   <input type="checkbox">Frosting<br>

14   <br>

15   <button>Order!</button>

16   </html>
```

← Add another option for customers.

Add three checkboxes for sprinkles, ice cream, and frosting. Type <br> after each one to make the next element start on a new line.

← Move the next element to a new line.

← Add an order button to your page.

Unlike the drop-down, the checkboxes allow you to choose more than one thing.

documents/store.html

Click 'n' Cake
Choose your flavor

Vanilla ▼
Choose the toppings

☐ Sprinkles
☑ Ice cream
☑ Frosting

Order!

STEP 6: See the changes

Save your work again, then refresh your web page.

EXPERIMENT

Make more cake flavors and more toppings.

Let customers choose from small, medium, or large cake sizes. Will you use a drop-down or checkboxes for this?

Use the code from page 12 to add a picture of a cake to the page.

Links and Photos

Let's go back to your favorites page and add some pictures. We will need to use the **<img>** tag. Once these are working, we will add some links to other websites with the **<a>** anchor tag.

documents/fav.html

My Favorite Things
Sports:

STEP 1: Open your fav.html file

Start your text editor.

Click File>Open and browse to find **fav.html** (this is the file you created on page 10).

STEP 2: Locate an image

Search for a picture to go with your page, or visit **maxw. com/graphics**.

Save image
Copy image
Copy image address

Right-click on the image and choose Copy **Image Address**.

Soccer clipart

We aren't copying the actual picture, just where it is—the address or URL.

STEP 3: Make space

```
5  <p>Soccer</p>  |
```

Click at the end of the line where you want to add your picture.

```
5  <p>Soccer</p>
6
```

Press the enter key to make a gap.

```
5  <p>Soccer</p>
6
```

Click at the start of line 6 again.

STEP 4: Add the picture code

```
5  <p>Soccer</p>
6  <img src='https://maxw.com/graphics/ball.png'>
```

Type **<img src='**   Paste in the picture address.   Type **'>**

img is short for image, src is short for source.

Ctrl **V**

On a PC, hold down the **Control** key, and tap "**V.**"

cmd ⌘ **V**

On a Mac, hold the **Command** key then tap "**V.**"

STEP 5: Save the page

■ Click **File > Save**.

■ Type **fav2.html** as the file name.

STEP 6: View your page

- Open your documents folder and double-click on the **fav2.html** file.

documents/fav2.html

My Favorite Things
Sports:

STEP 7: Resizing pictures

If you chose a large picture, then you will need to resize it.
Add the width attribute to your img tag, and set its size in pixels.

```
6  img src='https://maxw.com/graphics/ball.png' width='150px'>
```

Save your work again, then refresh your web page.
See step 5 on page 11 for help.

EXPERIMENT

Try changing the width from 150 to larger or smaller values. Repeat steps 2-4 to add more pictures.

Now add some links to your favorite websites.

STEP 8: Visit a website

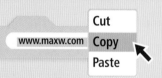

www.maxw.com

Visit a website.

www.maxw.com

Click the address to highlight it.

www.maxw.com

Cut
Copy
Paste

Right-click the address and choose **Copy**.

STEP 9: Add a link to the site

Decide where to add your link and make some space (see box 3).
Type in this code:

```
13  <a href='https://maxw.com/'>Coding Books</a>
```

Type `<a href='`   Paste the address.   Type `'>Coding Books</a>`

Books:
Coding Books

Your link will appear with a line underneath it.

Save your work again, then refresh your web page.

href is short for hypertext reference.

Posting photos on social media—How it works

Turn to page 30 for information of how to use social media safely and securely.

1. A photo is taken.

2. An app is used to post (send) it to a social media website.

3. It gets uploaded to the server that hosts the website.

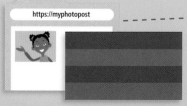

https://myphotopost

4. HTML Code is generated to show the picture in a web page.

5. The photo poster's friends will see the picture when they visit the social media site.

6. If the photo was posted publicly, it will be seen by anyone searching for certain #hashtags.

17

JavaScript and Interaction

We've seen how HTML can be used to display things on web pages. But how do we make things happen? How do we make buttons work?

To make a web page interactive, we need to add a second coding language called JavaScript. A script section is added to the page of code to contain the JavaScript. Let's start by making a simple dice program.

Making a simple dice program

To make the program, we will add an `<h1>` heading and a button to the page. When the button is clicked, it will run a function called throwDice.

```
<button onclick="throwDice()">Throw</button>
```

Add a button.

The event that we will be listening out for—a click.

The function that will run when the button is clicked.

What will be shown on the button.

End of the button tag.

We also need to give the heading tag a name.

The id attribute is how we set the name of an element.

Our id (name) is **dice**.

```
<h1 id="dice">
```

This is how to use the script element.

This shows the start of some JavaScript.

```
<script>
</script>
```

This shows the end.

Finally we need some JavaScript to show the number.

This selects the dice element so we can make changes to it.

This is where we make it display the dice value.

```
document.getElementById("dice").innerHTML=d;
```

We will create our own **function** called **throwDice**, which simulates throwing a die. A function is a section of code that does a particular task. We will also use some ready made functions, **random** and **floor**.

This function will pick a random number between 0 and 1.

And this function will round down a number (so 2.5 would be 2).

```
random()          floor()
```

18

■ STEP 1: Start a new HTML file
Start your text editor or click **File > New**.

■ STEP 2: Enter the code
Type this code into your text editor.

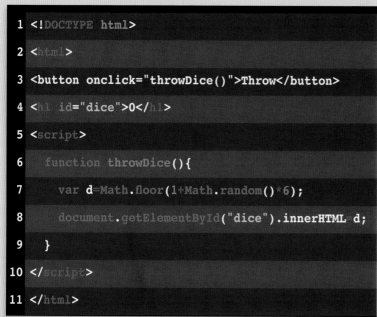

```
1  <!DOCTYPE html>
2  <html>
3  <button onclick="throwDice()">Throw</button>
4  <h1 id="dice">0</h1>
5  <script>
6    function throwDice(){
7      var d=Math.floor(1+Math.random()*6);
8      document.getElementById("dice").innerHTML=d;
9    }
10 </script>
11 </html>
```

Set the document type.

Start the HTML page.

Add a button to the page.

Add a heading called dice, showing 0.

Start the script section.

Define the **throwDice** function.

Create a variable called **d**. Generate a random number between 1 and 6 and store it in the variable. Show the value of the variable in the heading called **dice**. The * is how you multiply in JavaScript.

End of the function.

End of the script section.

End the web page.

■ STEP 3: Save the page

- Click **File > Save**.
- Go to your documents folder.
- Type **dice.html** as the file name.

A variable is a part of the program that can store a value. Unlike a normal number, the value of a variable can change.

Click the button to throw the die.

■ STEP 4: Test it
Open your documents folder and double-click the **dice.html** file.

documents/dice.html

Throw
3

■ EXPERIMENT
Change the color of the die. Can you change the color of the button too?

Make a second die: add a second heading. Call it dice2. Make another variable called d2. Add some code to give it a random value between 1 and 6.

Moving Around

Let's learn how to make a simple game. We will start by adding a picture of a helicopter to a page. Some JavaScript will make it move when a key is pressed.

To keep things organized, more complex HTML pages are split into two sections.

```
<head>
..
</head>

<body>
..
</body>
```

← The head

← The body

In this project, we won't use the head section. We will use the body tag and set its background color.

We need to make things happen when we press keys on the keyboard. We will add something called an event listener to check for any keys being pressed.

The web page.

The **event** that we will be "listening" out for—a key press.

The **function** that will run when a key is pressed.

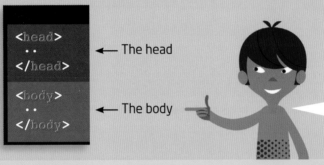

```
document.onkeydown=moveHeli;
```

Different codes are sent when keys get pressed.

Key:	Code:
←	37
↑	38
→	39
↓	40

We can position the helicopter by setting its left and top properties. They are measured in pixels (px).

Top

Left

Before we can set left and top properties, we need to set the position attribute to absolute like this:

```
style="position:absolute;"
```

If you don't set the position to absolute, the left and top attributes will be ignored.

STEP 1: Download an image

helicopter clipart

Search for **helicopter clipart** or visit **maxw. com/graphics**.

Right-click the image and click **Save File As**.

STEP 2: Move the image

Find the **heli.png** file and drag it to your My Documents folder. (On a Mac drag it to Documents.)

Downloads

heli.png

heli.png

heli.png

My documents

STEP 3: New file

Start your text editor or click **File > New**.

STEP 4: Type in the code

Type this code into your text editor.

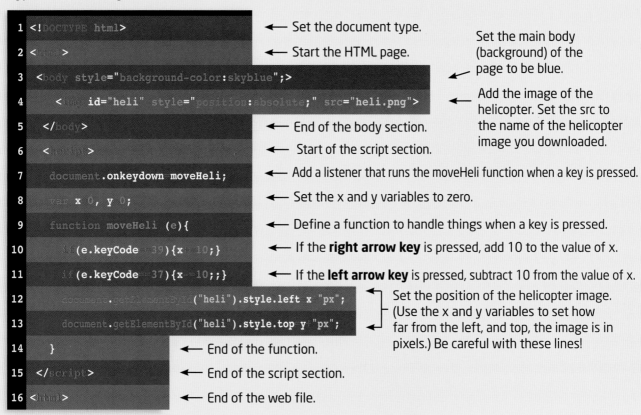

```
1   <!DOCTYPE html>
2   <html>
3   <body style="background-color:skyblue";>
4     <img id="heli" style="position:absolute;" src="heli.png">
5   </body>
6   <script>
7   document.onkeydown moveHeli;
8   var x 0, y 0;
9   function moveHeli (e){
10    if(e.keyCode  39){x  10;}
11    if(e.keyCode  37){x  10;;}
12    document.getElementById("heli").style.left x "px";
13    document.getElementById("heli").style.top y "px";
14  }
15  </script>
16  <html>
```

← Set the document type.

← Start the HTML page.

Set the main body (background) of the page to be blue.

Add the image of the helicopter. Set the src to the name of the helicopter image you downloaded.

← End of the body section.

← Start of the script section.

← Add a listener that runs the moveHeli function when a key is pressed.

← Set the x and y variables to zero.

← Define a function to handle things when a key is pressed.

← If the **right arrow key** is pressed, add 10 to the value of x.

← If the **left arrow key** is pressed, subtract 10 from the value of x.

Set the position of the helicopter image. (Use the x and y variables to set how far from the left, and top, the image is in pixels.) Be careful with these lines!

← End of the function.

← End of the script section.

← End of the web file.

STEP 5: Save

■ Click **File > Save**.

■ Go to your documents folder.

■ Type **heli.html** as the file name.

STEP 6: Test it

Open your documents folder and double-click on the **heli.html** file.

documents/heli.html

Click the helicopter, then use the left and right arrow keys to fly around.

EXPERIMENT

Add more code to make the helicopter move up and down.

Try using a different image instead of the helicopter.

RGB Color Sliders

On page 12 we set the page color by using "background-color:red." But what if we want dark red or red with a touch of orange? To do this, web pages mix colors using a system called RGB codes.

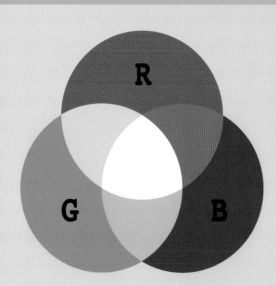

RGB stands for Red, Green, and Blue. A color is mixed by combining red, green, and blue light. The amount of each color is set by choosing a value between 0 and 255.

To make pure red, we would set the R value to 255. We wouldn't need any blue or green, so the code for red is **rgb(255,0,0)**.

To make purple, we need some red, no green, and some blue. So the code is **rgb(120,0,120)**.

The RGB color system can mix over 16 million colors!

Let's build a page that has three sliders—for red, green, and blue.

The sliders set the RGB code, changing the page color.

documents/sliders.html

rgb(255,0,128)

STEP 1: Start a new HTML file

Start your text editor or click **File > New**.

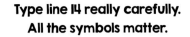

STEP 2: Type in your code

Type this into your text editor.

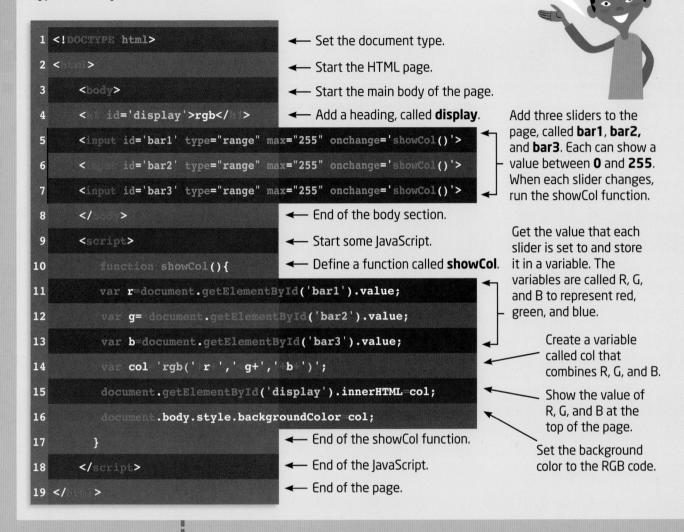

```
1  <!DOCTYPE html>
2  <html>
3    <body>
4      <h1 id='display'>rgb</h1>
5      <input id='bar1' type="range" max="255" onchange='showCol()'>
6      <input id='bar2' type="range" max="255" onchange='showCol()'>
7      <input id='bar3' type="range" max="255" onchange='showCol()'>
8    </body>
9    <script>
10     function showCol(){
11       var r=document.getElementById('bar1').value;
12       var g= document.getElementById('bar2').value;
13       var b=document.getElementById('bar3').value;
14       var col='rgb('+r+','+g+','+b+')';
15       document.getElementById('display').innerHTML=col;
16       document.body.style.backgroundColor=col;
17     }
18   </script>
19 </html>
```

← Set the document type.

← Start the HTML page.

← Start the main body of the page.

← Add a heading, called **display**.

Add three sliders to the page, called **bar1**, **bar2**, and **bar3**. Each can show a value between **0** and **255**. When each slider changes, run the showCol function.

← End of the body section.

← Start some JavaScript.

← Define a function called **showCol**.

Get the value that each slider is set to and store it in a variable. The variables are called R, G, and B to represent red, green, and blue.

Create a variable called col that combines R, G, and B.

Show the value of R, G, and B at the top of the page.

Set the background color to the RGB code.

← End of the showCol function.

← End of the JavaScript.

← End of the page.

STEP 3: Save your page

- Click **File > Save**.
- Go to your documents folder.
- Type **sliders.html** as the file name.

STEP 4: Test your page

Open your documents folder and double-click the **sliders.html** file.

documents/sliders.html

rgb(165,222,153)

EXPERIMENT

Move the sliders to make red. Try to make different shades of red, from bright to dark red. What do you notice about how the RGB code changes?

Move the sliders to try and make black. Now try and make white. How about different shades of gray?

Search Engines

We use search engines every time we want to look for information online or find a website about a specific subject. But how do they work? How do search engines like Google know where everything is?

Web crawlers

A "web crawler" or "spiderbot" starts by looking at every single web page it can find. The web crawler makes a copy of every page it finds as it crawls over the entire web.

One site completed. Only 2.1 billion more to go . . . better get going!

Lists and indexes

A book index lists the page number that a topic appears on. The search engine lists the website that the word appears on.

The search engine then looks at every page that has been found by the web crawler. It goes through each one and starts making an index—a list of words that show up on the web page.

This is just like the index that you find in the back of a book. However, instead of just indexing the main theme on a page, most search engines make a list of almost every single word that shows up on the page.

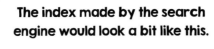

The index made by the search engine would look a bit like this.

```
{word: "news," website:"www.cnn.com"},
{word: "weather," website:"www.weather.com"},
{word: "tv," website:"www.tvguide.com"},
{word: "sports," website:"www.espn.com"},
{word: "books," website:"www.amazon.com"},
{word: "childrens'," website:'www.petersonsbooks.com"},
{word: "usa," website:"www.usa.gov"},
```

The search box

A web page is then built with a search box. Anyone visiting the web page types what they are looking for in the box and clicks "Search."

The search engine then looks through the list to find the word. Any sites containing the word are then shown to the user.

Server farms

Search engines may need to answer 50,000 queries every second! People expect the search engine to be very quick or they will stop using it. The search index the engine uses will also be very big—and get bigger every day.

To handle all this, thousands of computers are needed. These computers are housed in special buildings called data centers or server farms.

Better searching

Over time, search engines become more sophisticated. They have started to take note of other factors. These include how many times a word shows up on a page, how many other pages point to that page, and various other calculations.

Companies that run search engines are fairly secretive about the algorithms they use to rank each page and put them in order. Most also allow advertisers to pay to appear at the top of search results.

Now you know how search engines work, turn the page and start building your own!

Code a Search Engine

See pages 9–11 for help with starting a new HTML document.

STEP 1: Start a new HTML file

Type in the HTML below to create a search box and button on your web page.

```
1   <!DOCTYPE html>
2   <html>
3     <input id='searchbox'>
4   <button>Search</button>
5   </html>
```

← Set the document type to HTML.

← The start of the web page.

← Add an input box called searchbox.

← Add a button with a caption saying Search.

The end of the web page.

STEP 2: Save your page

- Click **File > Save**.
- Go to your documents folder.
- Type **search.html** as the file name.

STEP 3: Test your page

Double-click the **search.html** file in your documents folder.

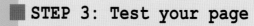

documents/search.html

search

Your web page should look like this.

To keep things simple we won't use a web crawler to look at all 2.1 billion sites. We'll start with just three, www.youtube.com, www.wikipedia.org, and www.cnn.com.

STEP 4: Add some data

Click after **</button>** and press **Enter** to make some space. Insert the new code from line 5 to 11.

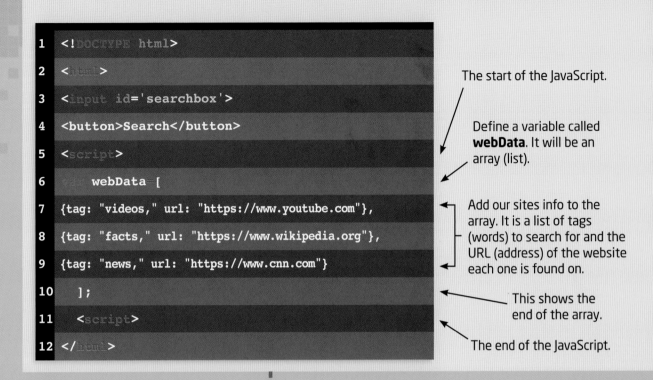

```
1    <!DOCTYPE html>
2    <html>
3    <input id='searchbox'>
4    <button>Search</button>
5    <script>
6      webData=[
7    {tag: "videos," url: "https://www.youtube.com"},
8    {tag: "facts," url: "https://www.wikipedia.org"},
9    {tag: "news," url: "https://www.cnn.com"}
10     ];
11     <script>
12   </html>
```

The start of the JavaScript.

Define a variable called **webData**. It will be an array (list).

Add our sites info to the array. It is a list of tags (words) to search for and the URL (address) of the website each one is found on.

This shows the end of the array.

The end of the JavaScript.

STEP 5: Test your page

Click **File > Save** in the text editor, then refresh your browser.

Now we need to plan some code that will do the searching.

Let's use a loop to check each word in the list. Put all this code in a function that runs when the button is clicked.

When "search" button is clicked:

- ■ Check if the word in the search box is the same as the first tag.
- ■ Check if it is the same as the 2nd.
- ■ Check if it is the same as the 3rd.
- ■ If it is the same as one of them, then show the URL of the website.

27

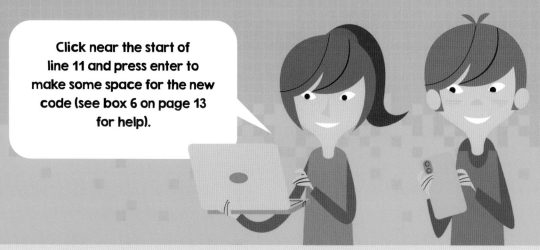

Click near the start of line 11 and press enter to make some space for the new code (see box 6 on page 13 for help).

STEP 6: The search function

Type in the code in lines 11–17, and edit line 4. This will make the search button work.

```
1  <!DOCTYPE html>
2  <head>
3  <input id='searchbox'>
4      <button onclick='doSearch(searchbox.value)'>Search</button>
5      <script>
6      var webData [
7          {tag: "videos," url: "https://www.youtube.com"},
8          {tag: "facts," url: "https://www.wikipedia.org"},
9          {tag: "news," url: "https://www.cnn.com"}
10         ];
11     function doSearch(x){
12         for(n 0; n webData.length; n ){
13             if(x webData[n].tag){
14                 document.write('<a href="' webData[n].url
                       '">' webData[n].url '</a>')
15             }
16         }
17     }
18     </script>
19 </html>
```

Edit line 4 to make it run the **doSearch** function when the button is clicked.

This passes what has been typed in the search box to the function.

The function stores what has been typed in a variable called **x**.

← Define a function called **doSearch**.

← Check to see if **x** matches one of the tags.

Start a loop to look through each item in the **webData** array.

← If it does, then add a link to the web page. The link will take us to the matching website.

← End of the if statement.

← End of the for loop.

← End of the **doSearch** function.

28

STEP 7: Save and refresh

Click **File > Save**. Refresh your browser to see the changes.

STEP 8: Test it

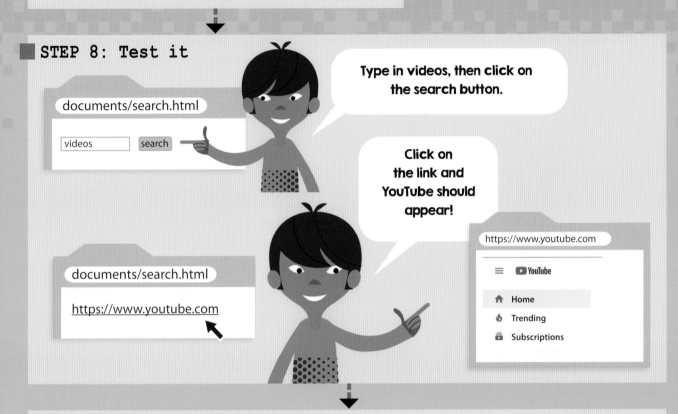

documents/search.html

videos   search

Type in videos, then click on the search button.

Click on the link and YouTube should appear!

documents/search.html

https://www.youtube.com

https://www.youtube.com

☰ ▶ YouTube

🏠 Home

🔥 Trending

▣ Subscriptions

STEP 9: Add more websites

Once you have got the search engine working, think of some more websites to include. You'll need to add a tag and a URL. Use lines 7–9 to remind yourself how the code needs to look.

Type the line really carefully.

```
{tag: "coding," url: "https://www.maxw.com"}
```

Add more lines of tags and URLs to the webData array. Test your code after each line by saving your code and refreshing your browser.

▮ EXPERIMENT

Make your search page look more colorful. Look back through the book to get ideas on how to change the button and add an image.

Change the results page. Add **document. write("<h2>Search results:</h2>");** at the start of the search function. What other code would you add there?

Glossary

attribute extra information about an HTML element, such as src

bit a unit of information in a computer that must be either 0 or 1

bug an error in a program that stops it working properly

data information in an electronic form that can be stored and used by a computer

data packet a small amount of data containing part of an image or some text, sent over the Internet

debug removing bugs (or errors) from a program

element an object on an HTML page such as a heading or image

event something that has happened while a program is running, such as a button being clicked or a key being pressed

function lines of code in a program that do a specific task, represented by a code word

hardware the wires, chips, sensors, and physical parts of a system or computer

HTML (Hyper Text Markup Language) the language used to create web pages

IP address (Internet Protocol address) a number that is given to each computer when it is connected to the Internet

JavaScript the language used to add interaction to web pages and make things happen

network a group of two or more computers connected together to share data

pixel a tiny dot on a computer screen, combined in the thousands to display pictures

protocol a set of rules or agreements about sharing data

random a number that can't be predicted

RGB (Red, Green, Blue) a system of mixing colors used by HTML

right-click clicking the right mouse button

server a large and powerful computer used to host a website

software a computer program containing instructions written in code

tag code words in an HTML document surrounded by < and >

text editor a program or app used to create (and change) typed code

URL (Universal Resource Locator) the address of a website or file stored online

variable a value used to store information in a program that can change

web browser a program or app used to view web pages, such as Google Chrome

Using social media safely

Social media is a great way for adults to communicate with people they know online. They can share photos and keep in touch even if they live a long way away. Most social networks have a mimimum age of 13 or 16.

A photo shared on a social network can end up being seen by almost anyone. Privacy settings will give some control over who can see things, but you can never be sure who will read or see what is posted.

It's also hard to be sure who people really are online. Some people may be pretend to be someone they are not. So be careful if you share messages or use online chat while you are playing games.

If you do experience anything that makes you feel uncomfortable, talk to your teacher, a parent, or an adult that you trust.

Bugs & Debugging

When you find your code isn't working as expected, stop and look through each command you have put in. Think about what you want it to do and what it is really telling the computer to do. If you are entering one of the programs in this book, check that you have not missed a line. Some things to check:

Correct code:	Common mistakes:	Notes:
`<h1>Sports</h1>`	`<h1>Sports` `<h1>Sports<h1>`	Missing end tag Missing slash /

`<input type="checkbox">`	`<input type='checkbox">`
	`<input type=checkbox">`
	`<input type="checkboxs">`
		Quote marks don't match "'
		Missing opening quote mark
		Spelling mistake

`<img src="ball.png">`	`<img src="ball">`
	`<img src='ball.png">`
	`<img src="BALL.PNG">`
		Missing file type .png
		Quote marks don't match "'
		Capital letters

`style="color:red;"`	`style="colour:red;"` `style:"color=red;"`	Spelling mistake : and = wrong way round
`Math.floor(1+Math.random()*6)`	`Math.floor(1+Math.random*6)` `Math.floor(1+Math.random())*6`	Missing brackets Number in wrong place

`var col='rgb('+r+','+g+','+b+')';`	`var col='rgb(+r+','+g+','+b+')';`
	`var col='rgb'('+r+''+g+','+b+')';`
	`var col='rgb'('+r+','+g+','+b'+)';`
		Missing quote '
		Missing comma ,
		' and + wrong way around

Tips to reduce bugs: When things *are* working properly, spend time looking through your code so you understand each line. Experiment and change your code, try out different values. To be good at debugging, you need to understand what each part of your code does and how your code works.

Practice debugging! Make a very short program and get a friend to change just one part of it while you aren't looking. Can you fix it?

If you are making your own program, spend time drawing a diagram and planning it before you start. Try changing values if things don't work, and don't be afraid to start again—you will learn from it.

Index

Further information

Get Ready to Code: Building a Website
by Alexa Kurzuis (Children's Press, 2019)

Creating a Web Site: Design and Build Your First Site!
by Greg Riksby (For Dummies, 2017)

Get Coding!: Learn HTML, CSS & Java Script & Build a Website, App & Game
by Young Rewired State (Candlewick, 2017)